SO, YOU THINK YOU WANT TO BUY A FRANCHISE?

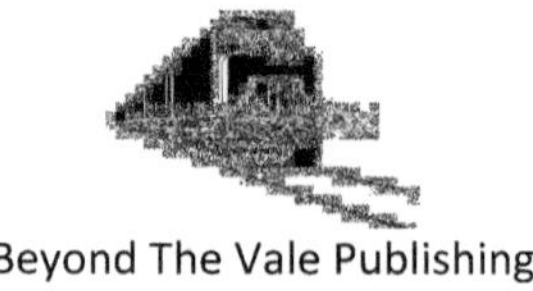

Richard James Edwards

SO, YOU THINK YOU WANT TO BUY A FRANCHISE?

To my wife who went through the journey with me and without
whom this book would not have been possible.

Contents

Contents continued

Introduction – so, you think you want to buy a franchise?

This book is written for anyone considering investing in a franchise business. It will look at most aspects of setting up, running and maintaining a franchise, as well as understand what a franchise is.

In it, we will look at both positive and negative aspects of all areas so that you, the reader, can decide whether a franchise is for you or not.

Inevitably, as with any business book, I will be using some jargon. I will keep this as clear as possible and I have put a guide at the back.

While this book is intended as a general guide to let you know more about the franchise process, every situation is unique and I would always recommend getting professional advice.

Why write this book?
As I write, it's August 2020, we're in the fifth month of lockdown and many people are being laid off from their jobs and there is uncertainty everywhere. Many of those are now considering "what next?" And there's no doubt buying a franchise is on some peoples list.

In June of 2016, my wife and I decided to buy a franchise. In August 2016, we brought a second shop. In April 2017, we closed the second shop and in June of 2017 we had sold the business at a huge loss. I'm not going to tell you which franchise it was, but I can tell you it was in the food sector.

I will be sharing some of our own personal franchising experiences so you can see how the theory translated into real life.

Franchise statistics
Franchising is big business. At the time of writing, the most up to date statistics about franchising were:
- In 2017, in the United States, there were around 733,000 franchise outlets, supporting nearly 7.6million jobs. That's around 3% of the economy.
- In South Africa in 2017, franchising accounted for 13.3% of all economic output.

What types of franchises are there?
The most popular is the food sector. I'm going to talk a lot about food chains in particular as that's my practical experience. The data will largely be transferrable to other franchises though.
Other popular types of franchises are:
- Retail
- Automotive
- Business services
- Home services
- Estate agents
- Internet sales
- Courier services

Have you ever had a conversation, or felt like this?

"Rough day?" The bartender looks at you as he hands the drink over. You take a sip.

"Awful," you catch sight of your reflection in the glass door of bar fridge. Your hair is a mess, shoulders slumped, shirt crumpled and a look in your eye that says, you just want to crawl under a rock.

You check the time on your phone. "Twelve hours at the office, slaving away for a pain in the ass boss, doing work I don't enjoy, for a business I don't even care about."

The bartender gives you a sympathetic look before taking your money off you and handing you change in coins small enough to ensure that you can leave a couple for him for his tip.

"I saw a guy in here last month, just the same as you," says the bartender. "He was moaning and complaining about his job too."

You look up from your drink.

"He kept saying how he had great ideas to improve the department but no one ever listened to him."

"Yeah, I can relate to that," you nod.

"In the end I stopped listening to him," the bartender shook his head.

You take a sip of your drink, it feels good, but then in the pit of your stomach comes that feeling. Tomorrow morning you have to get up, go back to work and do the same thing all over again.

"He had a plan, though," the bartender raised his eyebrows.

You sit up, ears pricked. Someone has a plan! There is a way to get out of this misery. "Tell me more," you urge the bartender.

"He was going to buy a franchise. He said that was his way out of the corporate world."

You take another sip from your drink. "A franchise," you say sitting up in your chair. "That's the way out, what a great idea."

You look around the bar and then back to the bartender. "What *is* a franchise?"

Chapter 1 – What is a franchise?

If you put that question into your favourite search engine, it will tell you that a franchise is:

"An authorization granted by a government or company to an individual or group enabling them to carry out specified commercial activities, for example acting as an agent for a company's products."

What that means is that a company, (the franchisor), will let you (the franchisee) use their brand, usually in return for a franchise fee.

 **What's in it for you?**

- You are running your own business, you are the boss (at least in theory, we'll come to that later).
- You get the right to use that company's branding for your business. The advantages of branding include:
  - Customer recognition.
  - Competitive edge – customers come to your brand.
  - Introducing new products is easier.
  - Customer loyalty.
  - Credibility.
- They will share with you their expertise and give you the necessary training for you to run your business.

- Large franchises will advertise nationally through the media, which you will benefit from.
- There will be other franchisees for you to network with.
- You are part of a larger business now, with which comes technical support from the franchisor.

What's in it for them?

- They get another branch, increasing their footprint without them having to lay out the money for it (capital expenditure).
- They will receive a franchise fee from you.
- Instead of employing a salaried manager, they have a business owner. A business owner will almost certainly be far more motivated than a manager to make sure that branch is a success. You want to invest money to make money, right?

So, it sounds like a real win-win scenario for both parties. You use their brand, pay them a fee and in return they have another branch being run by a motivated owner.

Why isn't everyone doing it?

Chapter 2 – Franchise or start your own business?

 "I've done it!" You smile at the bartender after another awful day at the office.

"What have you done?" he hands you your drink, and takes your money.

"I've researched franchises," you sit up in your chair. "There's hundreds to choose from. Food, education, DIY, car repairs, internet sales. Even pest control!"

"Sounds like you had a busy day," smiles the bartender as he puts your change and slip on the counter.

"They owed me a few hours," you say defensively as you pick up your glass.

"There was a woman in here the other day," the bartender leans over the bar. "She was telling me she started her own business a few months back and it was the best thing she ever did."

"A franchise?"

"No, she said she looked into but didn't fancy it. She opened her own business."

Crestfallen, you take a drink. Was that two hours internet surfing wasted. Maybe you should have worked on that presentation instead?

You look at the bartender. "But what's best? A franchise or your own business?"

 Let's look at the differences between franchising and starting your own business in some key business areas.

1. Branding

The design, name or symbol that identifies one business distinct from another. Just drive around any retail park and see how drawn you are to a shop/restaurant just because you see a particular shop name or logo.

1.1 Franchising

One of the most significant advantages of a franchise is you are buying a ready-made brand. The benefits of a good brand are mentioned in chapter 1. This will give you a massive push towards the holy grail of any business – customers. Customers are the key to any successful business, and will come to your business just because they recognise the brand.

Bear in mind though that while good experiences will reflect well on your business, equally, bad experiences will reflect poorly on your business. If someone has a complaint against your brand on social media because the branch down the road did something wrong, this will reflect negatively on your business too.

1.2 Your own business

Creating a brand is something that can take years and a significant amount of investment. It may mean using a marketing firm, coming up with a strategy, pouring money into advertising and hours of time self-promoting on social-media.

The advantage to you is that having done that, it is yours. You decide the colour scheme, mission statement, target market and quality of your product.

2. Suppliers

Whether setting up a restaurant, pest control, automotive or any other type of business, you need to ensure you buy good quality products from reliable, reputable and value for money suppliers. This, after all, is what you will be re-selling to your customers.

2.1 Franchising

All the suppliers will be ready and waiting. Tried, tested and accepted for quality. And there may even be special rates and discounts arranged for your franchise.

2.2 Your own business

You may be starting from scratch, although you're likely to have some contacts. Just take a minute to think of how many suppliers a food outlet would need. Not just the obvious ones like the food and drink providers, but the less obvious ones like, printing for the menus, takeaway containers, cleaning products, cutlery and crockery, pest control, wifi, point of sale systems, stationery, even table cloths. The list is a long one and finding reasonable priced and reliable suppliers can be difficult and time consuming.

Either way, as a new business or a new franchise, it is unlikely that suppliers will grant credit, meaning that in the beginning, you will more than likely have to buy on a cash on delivery basis. We'll talk more about your cash outlay in chapter 6.

3. Advertising

You need to get the word out there, you have a great product and the public need to know.

3.1 Franchising

There's likely to be an advertising fund which the franchisor will collect and use to spend on promoting the franchise nationally. It may be through TV or radio, billboards or sponsorship. You receive the benefit of economies of scale and may have a greater presence in the market place as a result. It is still likely that you will be responsible for local advertising.

3.1 Your own business

You will have to do your own advertising. You have the freedom of choice as to when/where that advertising happens, but it does mean you are responsible for deciding where and how to advertise your business.

You will have the freedom to set your own advertising budget though.

4. Operating hours

You're the boss, you want to set your own hours, right? Wrong!

4.1 Franchising

Operating hours are likely to be prescribed by the franchisor, although if you have a shop in a mall, you may be subject to the landlord opening times.

4.2 Your own business

You will have more freedom to decide what operating times you have, again you may have to check with the landlord if you have retail premises.

If you have a working from home business, then you have the freedom to choose your own hours, but remember the old saying – you get more out if you put more in.

5. Look and feel
As a retailer, food outlet or even automotive franchise, a nice welcoming space for your customers is important.

5.1 Franchising
Franchisors will require all their retail outlets to have the same look and feel as it forms an integral part of their brand. Thus, concept and design are likely to be taken out of your hands. This will also include the uniform.

5.2 Your own business
You have the freedom to choose your own décor and to what standard that décor is maintained to. Obviously though, if your tiles are cracked and your lights don't work, you're likely to drive customers away.

6. Pricing
What are you going to sell your goods and services for?

6.1 Franchises
Many franchises will expect you sell their product for the same price no matter where you are in the country. This is despite costs, in particular shop rentals, being widely different depending where you are based.

6.2 Your own business
The selling price is entirely up to you. There are many factors to consider though. We will look at these further in the gross profit chapter, chapter 7.

7. Location
If you have any kind of retail business then location is all important.

7.1 Franchises

A franchise will have set criteria as to where locations can operate. Having too many of the same type of brand in a small area would not make business sense as they would be competing against each other. This will vary depending on type of franchise. You're likely to need more restaurants in an area than tyre repair shops for example.

7.2 Your own business

You have freedom to choose where you want to work. Choice is important as you need enough customers to sustain you. You can choose that mall close to home, but consider competition, accessibility and foot traffic through the mall.

8. Expertise

You're going to be self-employed, but how much do you really know about the business you're going in to?

8.1 Franchising

Your franchisor will likely give you a training course. They will have experts at head office to help and you will be able to contact other franchisees and ask for their opinion. You should be well supported.

8.2 Your own business

Here you are likely to be dependent on your own knowledge and experience gained over the course of your working life. This may restrict you to the type of business you can run. If you've been a mechanic for twenty years, for example, setting up a florist shop may involve a learning curve.

Ultimately though, you know your strengths and have the freedom to choose a business based on those.

9. Being your own boss

How much freedom will you really have?

9.1 Franchising

You will be your own boss to a certain extent. There are likely
to be rules, restrictions and requirements in place by the
franchisor and sometimes it will feel as if you work for them.

9.2 Your own business

As it says in the subtitle above, this is your business and so
you are your own boss, with the freedom to make whatever
business decisions that you feel are in the best interests of
your business. Remember though that ultimately pleasing the
customer is your objective, technically making them the boss.

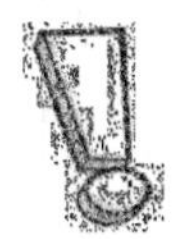

Our personal experience
We purchased in a fairly small franchise, around
fifty shops at the time. A quick internet search tells
me there are fewer now. The franchisor was the
founder and we felt that being involved in a smaller franchise
would give us more support, as we were a bigger cog in a
smaller machine.

We were wrong.

In reality, the founder was far too involved in the business
and seemed unable to let go of any control and as a result felt
like our boss – one of the worst bosses we ever had.

The head office, which we thought would offer us support
was woefully undermanned and under skilled, providing us
with little or no support. The training was inadequate, we
didn't feel ready to run our own franchise.

We were provided with a large list of suppliers and spent
many hours completing application forms for new accounts.

We paid 2.5% of our turnover towards a marketing fund,
which we were told was fully used. Despite this assurance, we

never saw or heard an advert, a billboard or any other form of marketing outside of a Facebook page.

I know what you're thinking – who can't set up a Facebook page?

Chapter summary

The table below summarises the relative advantages and disadvantages of a franchise compared to setting up your own business:

FRANCHISE	YOUR BUSINESS
Advantages	**Advantages**
The brand	Your profit is yours (after tax)
Expertise of head office	Freedom to choose:
National advertising	Price
Network of other owners	Location
Suppliers are established	Style
Training provided	Company ethic/mission statement
Disadvantages	**Disadvantages**
Franchise fee to pay	Build the business from nothing
Not your own boss	Find suppliers
There will be brand restrictions	Establish brand and customer base
Not in charge of pricing	More uncertainty
May be restrictions in location	You may not have the expertise

Chapter 3 – Which Franchise?

 "Well you look in a good mood this evening," the bartender compliments you as you head towards your usual seat and he reaches to the shelf and pours your drink.

"I feel good. I've made my decision. I can't take this corporate world any more with all the pressure I'm under and the stress that goes with it."

"That's why I'm a bartender," the bartender looks at you and smiles.

You sit down on the bar stool. "I've done it, I've decided to buy a franchise."

"Congratulations!" the bartender places your drink on the bar.

"I've weighed it all up. I'm going to leave my corporate job and buy a franchise. I've researched it. There are loads in the area available to buy. I won't have to deal with my boss, my deadlines or the traffic anymore."

"That's just great," the bartender reaches to the fridge to get a drink for another customer. "Which franchise are you going to buy?"

You stop, drink half way to your mouth. "I don't know. Which franchise *am* I going to buy?"

There are plenty of franchises to choose from and the decision of which one to buy is, in the end, something that is hugely personal. Some factors to consider are:

1. What are you interested in?

Running a franchise, like any other job will likely take up a lot of your time. You will end up working long hours, thinking about in your spare time and discussing it with your friends and family, so it's going to be best for you to pick something you're interested in.

In a perfect world, it would be best to pick a job that is also your hobby.

2. What are your skills and experience?

You are likely to have staff in your franchise. You will get more respect from them if you know more than they do. If you are a trained chef, then why not choose a restaurant. If you're a good teacher then look for something in an educational field. If you've never opened a car bonnet before then I would avoid motor repairs and if you've never used a power tool then I would probably avoid a DIY shop.

There are many food related franchises and we can't all be trained chefs, but a rudimentary knowledge of cooking would definitely be an advantage.

The franchisor will offer a basic training in whichever franchise you look at. It's in their interests that they ensure you have the necessary skills to be able to understand what the job entails.

3. What services do you enjoy?

Try and choose a franchise you enjoy visiting and making use of. That will give you an association with the brand. Having visited the franchise a few times may also give you some background into how it operates.

4. What's your budget and your expected return?
Available funds may be the limiting factor here. You might not be able to go straight for the 300-seater restaurant, or that Bentley dealership you like so much. But there's nothing wrong in starting small.

5. Can you see potential for the franchise?
Is the franchise you are interested in the 'next big thing'? Or is it the one you used to see on every street corner but now, not so much? A declining franchise footprint can indicate the public is losing faith with that brand or has a bad reputation amongst previous franchisees.

6. Still stuck? Then try some research.
My advice would be to research the existing franchises. What's missing from your neighbourhood? Look on line for reviews and feedback, maybe make a short list.

Then, get out and visit them in other locations. Look at how well run they are – for example are the staff friendly and enthusiastic? What state of repair is the premises in? Is it well stocked? Are they busy?

7. Still stuck after your research?
Then maybe franchising isn't for you after all. Look to a good life coach, who will help you find your purpose.

A good life coach will help you discover your true purpose and ensure you follow your dream and not a fantasy.

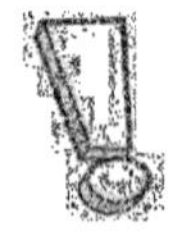

Our personal experience

My wife and I had set a budget and stuck to it. We went and chose in the food industry. Our reasoning was that we understood food, people eat and then the next day they get hungry and eat again, so it would be a ready-made daily demand. **We chose a daytime franchise because we didn't want to work in the evening.**

Our combined experience in food retailing was that I had spent nine months as a waiter when I was seventeen and my wife had run her own bagel shop for six months. And we eat out a lot.

We chose a franchise neither of us had visited or used before.

Equipped with four weeks training from the franchisor we went into our shop and needless to say we were utterly unprepared for it.

The result was that neither of us enjoyed it.

Chapter summary

Choosing the right franchise for you is something personal, but consider:

- Services you enjoy using as a customer,
- Your interests and skills,
- Your budget,
- Can you see a future for that franchise?

Chapter 4 – New or used?

 "I know which franchise I'm going to buy," you tell the bartender a few weeks later.

"Well done!" The bartender pushes your drink across to you.

"XYZ. They've got a great reputation and my wife and I love their products. I spoke to them and they're looking to open up a new outlet in the new mall. It's perfect."

"The owner of the XYZ in the *old* mall was in here yesterday. He's looking to sell his," the bartender replies.

You look at him open mouthed. You've been to that mall before. Both are about the same distance from your house.

"Which should I buy, the old one or the new one?" You take a sip of your drink, the bartender shrugs and goes and serves another customer.

 There are a number of factors to consider when deciding between a new and existing franchise.

1. Income
You're buying a franchise to make a return, so the bigger profit the better.

1.1 Existing franchise

They will likely have been trading for a while and so they should have some accounts available that you can look at. That will give you a feel for the franchise's historic performance. Current bank statements will give you a feel for how the business is performing, but they don't give the full picture. We will look more at how to interpret accounts in chapter 8.

1.2 New franchise

Obviously, there won't be historic accounts available, but the franchisor should be able to provide you with a reasonable estimate of the likely revenue based on similar sized branches in similar malls.

Yes, I know there's a lot of qualifiers in the previous sentence. Profitability projections are useful, but no one can tell the future, so they may be wrong.

2. Location

For a retail store, restaurant, or indeed any franchise with a bricks and mortar trading base, location is key. Here you need to assess who your likely customer would be and whether that kind of person visits that mall, shopping centre or that part of town.

Within the mall, you need to be easy to find and preferably in a busy part of the mall and not tucked down a side alley surrounded by closed shops where customers are unlikely to find you.

Consider also the competition around you and around the mall. As a restaurant being in a food court surrounded by other food outlets may not be a bad thing as hungry people will go to the food court, increasing your chance of customers.

Ask, where is the nearest other branch of your franchise? Is the mall busy? Are there future renovation projects? Are any new malls planned in the vicinity?

Even with non-retail businesses, consider who your customer is likely to be and how likely they are to be close to where you are.

2.1 Existing franchise

Pay it a visit. Go at different days at different times of day. It should be easy to assess whether or not the franchise is in a good location. Was it easy to find, is there plenty of passing traffic? Speak to the existing owners and staff to find out what they think to the location.

2.2 New franchise

Here will be slightly more speculation. The franchisor should be able to show you where they would like you, or they may just have a geographical area and the choice of location is down to you. Either way, do your homework and consider whether your likely customer is likely to come within a mile of where your business will be.

3. Staff

Employees can be your biggest asset, but they can also be a liability. Good staff give your customer an enjoyable experience. Rude, sloppy, lazy staff give your customer a bad experience and your franchise a bad reputation. There's more on staff in chapter 9.

3.1 Existing franchise

Some of the staff may have been working there for many years and that experience can be vital in helping you to manage the business. They may however have formed bad/lazy habits and may not perform to the standard expected by you or the franchisor.

Speak to the vendor and find out who the trouble makers are. Additionally, speak to the franchisor to see whether you are over or under staffed.

3.2 New franchise

The staff are all likely to be new as well. You will have to recruit them and have them trained. They are likely to work a little slower in the beginning, but will not come with the bad habits that existing staff may have.

4. Fixtures, fittings and equipment

Particularly if you are investing in a retail store, the fixtures and fittings will form a first impression for your customers.

4.1 Existing franchise

Scrutinise everything that will be transferred to you as part of the business. Insist on a report of everything that is broken and ask the vendor to replace or repair. If there are vehicles in the business then these will have to be road-worthied prior to the transfer.

Insist on replacement to chipped/cracked tiles and that the premises is painted. Although you are buying a used franchise, you want that franchise to look as good and be as well-equipped as it possibly can.

4.2 New franchise

The franchisor will have experience working with a contractor who will completely fit out your premises. This is known as a turnkey outfit – all you have to do to start your business is to turn the key. All your equipment should be brand new and in working order.

5. Previous performance

This is not financial, but rather the performance of the franchise in servicing its customers. The franchisor has built their brand on quality control criteria and performance standards and they will not want you to let the brand down.

This only applies to existing franchises. The franchisor should let you have information regarding any serious customer complaints or areas of concern.

6. Price

The all-important factor (speaking as an accountant) but also key because you're buying this as an investment to make a return.

6.1 Existing franchise

This will largely be calculated based on past profit performance, strength of the balance sheet, how much similar franchises have sold for or a combination. Failing that, the sellers have just made up a number to see how much they can get.

Often, like buying a house, the value is subjective. The true value being how much someone is willing to pay for it.

We will look further at valuing a business in chapter 5.

6.2 New franchise

The franchisor will have a fixed price for a new franchise and they should be able to show you a breakdown of how that figure is made up.

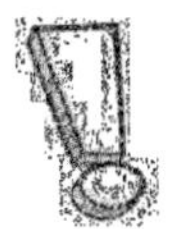

Our experience
The franchise my wife and I purchased was an existing franchise, largely delivery based and so the location aspect was not something we considered. It

was only when we had started operating that we appreciated how large the delivery area was.

This was a problem not only because of the cost involved but also the time. One delivery driver could be away for an hour at a time, placing pressure on the other drivers.

Generally speaking the staff we inherited were able to perform the job, although once we had purchased the store, the franchisor insisted that all the staff needed refresher training which the previous franchisee had not done. This was at our cost as the training was held at the franchisors premises and also left us short staffed.

We negotiated the selling price down from the asking price after a thorough review of other franchises for sale around the area.

We thought we were thorough in looking at the equipment to assess what was broken, but there were some problems we encountered almost straight away, running from having too few knives to a badly repaired fridge. One of the first things we had to buy was a new delivery motorbike. An expensive lesson learned.

Chapter summary

The table below summarises the relative advantages and disadvantages of investing in a new store compared to an existing franchise.

NEW FRANCHISE	EXISTING FRANCHISE
Advantages	**Advantages**
Some choice in where the franchise will be located	Proven track record of trading
You choose the staff	You can view and assess the location
Brand new fixtures, fittings and equipment	Experienced staff
Pay a fixed price based on franchisor calculations	You benefit from any goodwill the franchise has generated
Disadvantages	**Disadvantages**
Financial performance based on estimates	Any legacy of bad service will stay
Inexperienced new staff are likely to be slower	Staff may be complacent/have bad habits
Untried location	Old/worn fixtures, fittings and equipment
	Price you pay is highly subjective

Chapter 5 – How much to pay and how to raise the finance

"It's too much, it's too much," you mutter as you walk in to the bar.

The bartender nods as he pours you your overpriced drink. "I told you," he says.

"Not the drink," you tell him. "Although a discount would be nice."

You ignore the laugh from behind the bar.

"These franchises. They all seem to cost too much. How can I tell if it's value for money?"

Part 1 – how much to pay

1.1 Existing franchise

There are many different ways to value a business, some of them are extremely complicated and rely on projections. Some rely on historical data and some are little more than a guess. Let's start with the simpler ways.

- What did a similar franchise in a similar area sell for? Yes, not a great deal of thought or imagination gone into this one, but I suspect it happens a lot.

- The franchisor is likely to be experienced and will likely have a preferred method. In all probability, the franchisor will have helped the seller determine a price.

- You can take a multiple of the annual profit after tax (that's what's left after deducting all costs). Most industries have a standard which is most applicable to them, it maybe three times or even five times. For example, if the business made 10,000 profit after tax and the industry standard multiplier is five, then the business should cost 50,000.

- You can take the value of net assets. This means assets less liabilities. Assets that have a physical presence, (tangible) such as vehicles, shop fittings and computer equipment (but not stock – we'll talk about stock later) are relatively easy to value. What is more difficult is the value of the goodwill of the brand (intangible). How do you assess the number of extra customers you will receive because they like your brand?

- There may be a standard multiplier to apply to monthly turnover, maybe 1.5 or 2. Turnover is the total sales generated by the business exclusive of VAT. (We'll talk a bit more about VAT in chapter 6).

- Payback method. This is where you as the buyer have a preference as to how many years it will take you to recoup your investment. For example, if the business is expected to make 15,000 a year and you want to recoup your investment in 3 years, then the price you should pay is 15,000 x 3 = 45,000. This does rely on projections into the future which are highly subjective.

1.2 New franchise

The franchisor should have a price readily available for the cost of your new franchise. This will usually be the cost of the installations, shop fittings, equipment and sometimes other smaller items you will need to get you started, for example menus. This may vary depending on the size of the retail establishment you are looking at.

Part 2 – how can I assess if I'm paying too much?

Here are a few tools you can use to assess this, and compare franchise to franchise.

2.1 Profit

Cash is king and we're buying a franchise to make money.
Let's take a simple comparison of profit between 5 franchises:

Franchise	A	B	C	D	E
Profit	20 000	15 000	28 000	10 000	17 000

Based purely on these numbers, franchise C is the best one to buy

2.2 Factor in the cost of the franchise

Let's now factor in how much the franchise costs. Then we'll look at 2 assessment tools:

- Payback period – how many years will it take to have your money repaid?
- Return on investment (ROI). This is the profit divided by the investment and is expressed as a percentage.

Franchise	A	B	C	D	E
Profit	20 000	15 000	28 000	10 000	17 000
Investment	175 000	300 000	425 000	250 000	195 000
Payback (years)	8,8	20,0	15,2	25,0	11,5
ROI	11%	5%	7%	4%	9%

Now we can see that franchise A has the highest ROI at 11% and the shortest payback period – you get your cash back in 8 years and 10 months. Now franchise C is only third best.

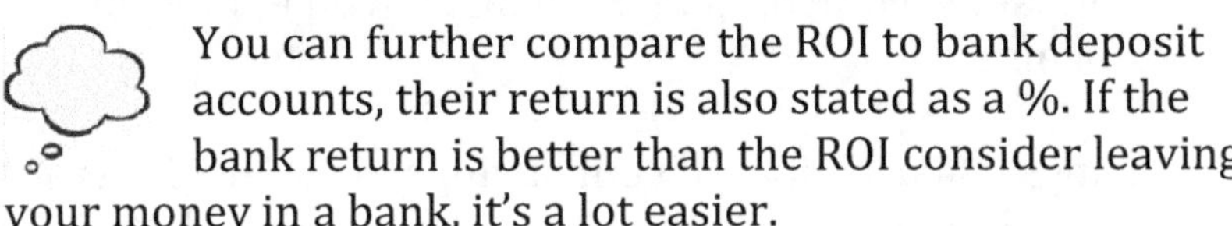

You can further compare the ROI to bank deposit accounts, their return is also stated as a %. If the bank return is better than the ROI consider leaving your money in a bank, it's a lot easier.

Remember, in most cases the profit doesn't include a salary for you, the profit is, in effect, your salary. This gives rise to an additional question – is 20,000 enough to support your lifestyle?

2.3 How do I know if the profit is right?

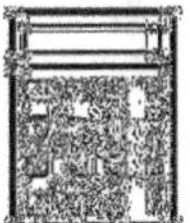

The accuracy of the profit figure quoted on the previous page is one of life's mysteries. If you're looking to buy an existing franchise then probably this will be last years figure, but how can you guarantee that profit will happen again? A new franchise and the profit figure will be an estimate from the franchisor. But how can you rely on an estimate? We will look more at profit and how to assess it yourself in chapter 8.

 More complicated methods of investment assessing include forecasting the profit forward and adjusting for inflation. Some of these are the Discounted Cash Flow and Net Present Value techniques and I mention for the sake of completeness. Future predictions are unreliable, complicated and time consuming. If you would like to explore further, I would recommend getting in touch with a professional.

Part 3 – financing the purchase of your franchise

 There are several options available to you to buy your franchise.

- Savings – take a dip into your savings. This is by far the easiest, but not always the best. Cash is king and it's always nice to know you have the security in your bank should things take a turn for the worse.

- Credit card. Quick and easy but expensive.

- Business loan from the bank. There may be requirements from the bank, such as business plans and cash flow projections. The bank wants to know the franchise will make enough money to repay their loan. Preparing a good business plan would be a book on its own. You may want to consider spending some time with your friendly neighbourhood financial planner or accountant.

- Borrow money from your friends and family. Many people, including me, would warn you against mixing business and pleasure. If you do go down this route, then do have a contract drawn up and ensure that both parties know what's expected of them.

- Franchisor funding. Don't be afraid to ask your franchisor whether they can fund you. They know the risks and returns of their business better than anyone.

3.1 Loan repayments and your accounts

If you borrow to fund your business, the loan repayment is split into two parts for your accounts:

- The interest. This is a cost and will show on your income statement.
- The capital repayment. The loan is a liability and does not appear on the income statement, instead it falls on the balance sheet. The capital repayments reduce the liability.

If you do borrow to fund your franchise remember the loan repayment will have to be made as well. The interest cost may not have been included in your franchisors estimates.

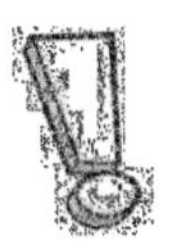

Our experience

The price we paid bore little resemblance to any of the pricing models I have mentioned above. It was a nice round sum that the franchisor had insisted on, as we were told by the agent. We did manage to negotiate a discount but even then, we still overpaid.

We were lucky enough to have savings available to us to buy the franchise, however I wouldn't recommend that you use all your savings to buy the franchise. Next time (if there is a next time) I would look to finance at least part of the purchase price and keep some cash.

They say cash is king. I don't know who 'they' are but they're definitely right. Besides, you're going to need some spare cash, as I will discuss in the next chapter.

Chapter summary

We've looked at the following:

- How to assess the value of your franchise:
  - New franchise – the franchisor should be able to provide a breakdown
  - Existing franchises are more complicated and may be subjective
- How to compare the relative financial performance of franchises.
- Ways in which you might finance the purchase of your franchise. Remember to factor in a loan repayment and interest into your calculations.

Chapter 6 – What is the franchise actually going to cost me?

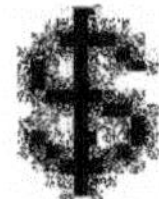

"Hello, I haven't seen you in here for a while. The usual?" the bartender looks up to you as you make your way across the bar and sit at a stool.

You nod in agreement and the bartender prepares your drink. "I've been busy," you say proudly. "Investigating a franchise, checking out the location and competition and deciding how to finance it."

"How much are you paying for it?" the bartender arches an eyebrow.

You look at him and see him mentally working out how much tip he can expect.

"It's a fair price. Five times profit after tax. It's in line with the industry standard."

The bartender nods his approval. "I heard there's a lot of costs associated with setting up a business."

"Really?" You ask. "What are they?"

Yes, that's right, prepare for the bills to come rolling in. These will also apply if you choose to set up your own business, with the exception of the franchise fee.

Franchise fee
There is likely to be a one-off signing up fee, which the franchisor will charge you. This will be to cover things like the

administration involved in set up and training. Be careful, the figure quoted may be exclusive of VAT, so you will have to add another 15% on top (rate from South Africa at the time of writing (July 2020)).

Stock

The price of stock will not be included in the purchase price of your franchise. You will have to stock up in addition to the cost of buying the franchise. After all, if you don't have stock, you have nothing to sell. If you have nothing to sell, you're less likely to make a profit.

If you're buying an existing franchise then the previous owner will sell you their stock. This means you'll have to attend a stocktake, where you count all the stock in the shop. Then you'll have to value the stock. The valuation should always be what it cost the previous owner to buy, excluding VAT rather than what the stock can be sold for. Expect to find yourself digging through invoices to make sure the prices are right. Make sure that the stock is usable and not out of date or unsaleable.

If you're buying a new franchise then you'll have to buy all the stock from scratch. This will mean you'll have to set up relationships with all the suppliers. Some of these may offer you credit facilities allowing you, usually, 7 days or 30 days to pay. Many will insist on cash in advance or on delivery if you're a new business with no credit history.

Lease deposits

If you are renting premises then expect to have to pay a deposit up front. Many landlords will expect you to give them three months rent as a deposit which will be refundable at the end of the lease. This is to cover the landlord against any potential default on your behalf.

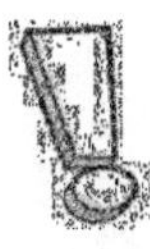

Our experience

The franchise fee, cost of stock and lease deposit added an additional nearly 25% on to the cost of buying the franchise.

Despite the fact I was expecting it, it was still a bitter pill to swallow.

Chapter summary

In this chapter we've discussed how much cash you will need to lay out to set your franchise up and running:

- The cost of your franchise,
- Plus all the stock you'll need to start it,
- Plus a lease deposit,
- Plus a one-off franchisor fee (if applicable).

Chapter 7 – What is gross profit and why is it so important?

"You're late tonight," the bartender says as he wipes down the bar.

"I've just been meeting with the franchisor," you say proudly. "Nice offices, they're obviously doing well. That's got to be a good sign, right?"

The bartender nods as he fixes your drink.

"They say I can expect a gross profit of 65%. That sounds really good."

"Does it?" says the bartender. "65% of what?"

You take a sip from your drink and look up. "I don't know."

So, this is the chapter where we first start looking at the numbers in some detail. (I'm an accountant, it had to happen sooner or later). Besides, remember you want your franchise to be profitable.

Gross profit
This is measured as turnover less cost of sales.

- Turnover is your total sales. This is how much cash you bring in.

- Cost of sales is how much it cost you to make those sales. It is calculated as opening stock/inventory plus purchases less closing stock/inventory.

Gross profit is often expressed as a percentage – gross profit divided by turnover. This is also sometimes referred to as your margin or gross margin.

If you're VAT registered, all these figures will exclude VAT. I'll talk more about VAT in chapter 8 part 6.

Example 1

Let's ignore stock to start with and pretend you buy a stationery retailers and you sell a stapler for 115 – that's 100 plus South African VAT, currently at 15%.

You buy the stapler from your wholesale supplier for 34.50 (30 plus VAT). Your gross profit is calculated as:

Turnover (sales)	100
Less cost of sales	30
Gross profit	**70**
Gross profit % (margin)	70%

Remember – the numbers above exclude VAT. That's simple enough. Let's look at something a little more complicated.

Example 2 – complicated cost of sales

Cost of sales will be more complicated where there is a process involved, for example if you sell a takeaway burger. All costs associated with the production of that burger will be included in that cost of sale.

For example:
- The bun,
- The patty,
- Lettuce,
- Mustard,
- Tomato/burger sauce,
- Packaging,
- Serviettes,
- The cost of delivery for all of the above,
- Even the gas and cooking oil you used to cook the patty.

To work out the cost of sales of that individual burger would be time consuming as the ingredients will come in bulk packages.

Then there's the question of how much of a lettuce do you put on a burger? 5%? 10%.

Your franchisor should have already done these calculations and know how much gross profit to expect on your biggest sellers and overall.

 **What about staff costs?**
Someone has to prepare the burger, shouldn't their cots be included as a cost of sale?

I would argue that yes, these are costs directly attributed to producing the burger and should be included. The franchisor that I was involved in disagreed and when she talked about gross profit it excluded staff costs. It's best to check with the franchisor what their definition of cost of sales is.

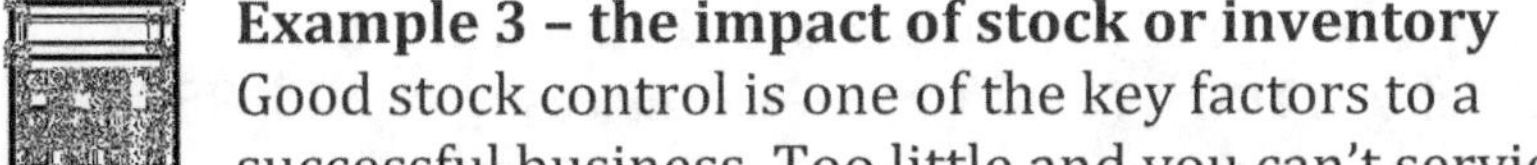

Example 3 – the impact of stock or inventory

Good stock control is one of the key factors to a successful business. Too little and you can't service your customers and you may miss out on that bulk discount. Too much and you restrict your cash flow and run the risk that the stock will perish, become obsolete or be stolen.

Stock valuation also has a major impact on your cost of sales.

For these next examples, we're going to look at monthly accounts.

3.1 Without a stock adjustment

Let's assume you're a stationery retailer again. A stapler won't perish and they can sit in stock for several months.

In January you start your business and buy a box of 100 staplers at 30 (excluding VAT). Your selling price is 100. Let's say in January, you sold 5. Excluding stock, your gross profit (in fact it's a loss) on staplers would look like this:

	January
Turnover - 5 at 100 each	500
Less cost of sales 100 at 30 each	3 000
Gross loss	**-2 500**
Gross loss	-500%

Based on sales and cost of sales alone, it would appear you have made a huge loss on sale of staplers. But, it's not a fair comparison – you have brought 100, but only sold 5, so you must have 95 in stock.

3.2 Adjusted for the value of stock

Let's assume you had none in stock to begin with and we value the stock at the cost to you – in this case 30. With 95 staplers in stock, we arrive back at 70% gross profit percentage as we did in example 1 earlier.

		January
Turnover - 5 at 100		500
Cost of sales:		
Opening stock	0	
Purchased 100 at 30	3 000	
Closing stock - 95 at 30	-2 850	
Total cost of sales		**150**
Gross profit		350
Gross profit % (margin)		70%

3.3 Opening stock adjustment

If closing stock reduces your cost of sales, then opening stock will increase your cost of sales.

Imagine we're now in February and you sell 12 staplers. With no adjustment for stock, your monthly accounts will look like this:

	January	February
Turnover - 5 / 12 at 100	500	1 200
Cost of sales - 100 / 0 at 30	3 000	0
Gross loss / profit	-2 500	1 200
Gross loss / profit %	-500%	100%

Let's show January and February with stock adjustments:

	January		February	
Turnover - 5 at 100		500		1 200
Cost of sales:				
Opening stock	0		2 850	
Purchased 100 at 30	3 000		0	
Closing stock - 95 at 30	-2 850		-2 490	
Total cost of sales		150		360
Gross profit		350		840
Gross profit % (margin)		70%		70%

- Note here that the opening stock for February is the same as January's closing stock.
- Note also that February's closing stock is now only 83 units (95 less 12 sold) at a cost of 30 each.
- In both cases, our gross profit % is 70%.

 **4. Stock control – how much stock should I have and how can I tell if it's too much?**

Stock is the life blood of your business, unless you're in the service sector. It can also make or break your business. Do you really want to go into your favourite franchise for lunch only to find out that the meal you really fancy is out of stock?

At the same time, do you want to find yourself unable to pay your rent or your staff because you have spent too much on stock?

4.1 How much cash should I tie up in stock?
Your franchisor should be able to help here and suggest an amount. You can calculate average stock holding days by looking at the accounts.

 Take the closing stock, divided by the annual turnover, multiplied by 365.
(If it's monthly turnover then multiply by 30).

So, if your annual turnover is 120,000 and your stock is 25,000 then 25,000 / 120,000 x 365 = 76 days.

This means your stock, on average sits on your shelves/in your warehouse for 76 days before being sold.

Or, in other words, your cash is tied up in stock for, on average 76 days.

 **4.2 Is 76 days too long, too short or about right?**

That depends on:

4.2.1 What industry are you in? For a restaurant it's too long, can you imagine eating a 76-day old tomato? For a car dealership, it may be about right.

4.2.2 How quickly can you get delivery of your product? If the wholesaler delivers weekly, then you only need 7- or 8-days' worth of stock. If you're importing and can only get the stock every 90 days, then you probably will need 90 days' worth of stock.

 **5. Why am I talking about gross profit and stock so much?**

- Turnover and cost of sales (the two numbers that make up the gross profit) should be the 2 biggest numbers on your accounts and therefore the most important.
- Cost of sales is what us accountants call a direct cost – it is directly related to your sales. To make a sale, you

have to incur a cost of sale. There is little you can do to reduce it (see below).

- You have to pay all your other costs, including a salary for you, out of the gross profit.
- Franchisors are likely to tell you what their expected gross profit margin is, so it's a useful tool to make comparisons. If franchise A has a gross profit of 70% and franchise B has 60%, then (in theory) there will be more money left over for everything else if you go for franchise A.

6. Are there any other things that will impact on the gross profit?

In the real world, you're unlikely to look at the gross profit on one item at a time as we have done previously. You will look at a combination of all your sales and all your cost of sales in the month.

Here are some factors that could make your gross profit percentage different from what the franchisor expects.

6.1 Your mix of sales is different from the franchisors standard model. You will sell a range of products and some products will naturally have a different gross profit margin.

6.2 Discounts, offers and promotions. These are especially prevalent in the food industry, where many franchises have special offers during quieter days of the week.

6.3 Bad stock control. This could mean stock becoming obsolete, damaged, out of fashion or, in the case of food, spoiling. This means you will have to heavily discount in order to sell, or even throw away. Bad stock control could also mean that your stock is going missing (employee theft – see section at the end of this chapter).

6.4 Seasonality. This is particularly true of the food industry, where fresh fruit and vegetables are not available locally produced and have to be imported and therefore there are seasonal price discrepancies.

6.5 Price increases from your suppliers. The franchisor will set the selling price so you have no control over that, and they may only change the prices once or twice a year. But your suppliers may increase their prices at any time throughout the year. A price increase on your best-selling product months after from the franchisors price increase will reduce your gross profit margin.

Our experience

We spoke with the franchisor before we took over and several times after we took over about gross margin. Each time she insisted that we should be able to obtain 65% gross margin. The best we ever managed was 58% and most months we were between 52% and 55%.

Let's put some numbers on that to give some context. If our turnover was 120,000 a month, then instead of an expected gross profit of 78,000 a month at 65%, our gross profit was 66,000 (at 55%). That's 12,000 less per month, which still had to pay for all the costs.

The franchisor put this down to bad stock management and theft. While I suspect that some of it was theft, there was very little stock wastage. I suspect each one of the five items listed above had a contribution to the much lower than expected gross profit.

With the benefit of hindsight, I should have spoken to other franchisors to assess what their actual gross profit margin was to check the franchisors claim.

Stock theft in the food industry
On top of staff eating food while they're working here are some interesting stories we heard during our time working in the food industry:

- Staff hiding food in their handbags.
- Staff hiding food around their person. I have heard tales of one lady who stuffed a whole frozen chicken down her pants.
- Throwing food in the garbage, only to retrieve it from the dumpsters at the end of the day.
- Concealing (packaged) bacon in a bucket of dirty mop water in order to retrieve the bacon when they went outside to tip the water down the drain.

Chapter summary
We've looked at gross profit, its importance and the factors that can affect it.

- Gross profit is sales less cost of sales.
- It's often shown as a % - gross profit divided by turnover
- It can be a useful tool in comparing franchises, but make sure the comparison includes the same costs.
- Gross profit is the cash from which all your other costs have to be paid.
- Why gross profit is sometimes different to expectations.
- Stock – how much should it be and how can I tell if it's too much?

Chapter 8 – Is it a good investment? Will the franchise make me money?

You pull your car into the car park, stamp on the brakes, get out and slam the door. You stomp towards the bar, brow heavily furrowed and a scowl on your lips.

"Drink?" asks the bartender. "You look like you could use one."

"Make it a double," you snap.

You're a good tipper, so the bartender doesn't take offence, and calmly places your drink on the bar. You snatch it and take a gulp.

"How's the franchise?" the bartender asks as he hands you the slip. "All that time and effort you put into the research, choosing the right franchise, the right location, I'm sure you must be raking in the money."

You look at him and snort. "Just had an argument with my partner," you shake your head. "Money, money, money, is all they think about. Not about the freedom that I have to run my own business."

The bartender nods sympathetically, before he short changes you.

"Will this franchise make money? Will we be able to pay the bills? Blah, blah, blah. That's all I ever get lately."

The bartender looks thoughtfully at you. "Will it make money?"

"The franchisor says it will," you pull a piece of paper from your pocket and unfold it. "Here's their projection, in black and white." You lay the paper on the bar and point to the bottom number. "Look it says it's going to make a profit."

"A projection," the bartender turns his head to look at the impressive number on the bottom of the page. "I projected that my favourite sports team would win last weekend," he nods his head.

"And did they?" you ask.

"No. They were useless," the bartender shrugs.

"So, how do I know that this projection is right?"

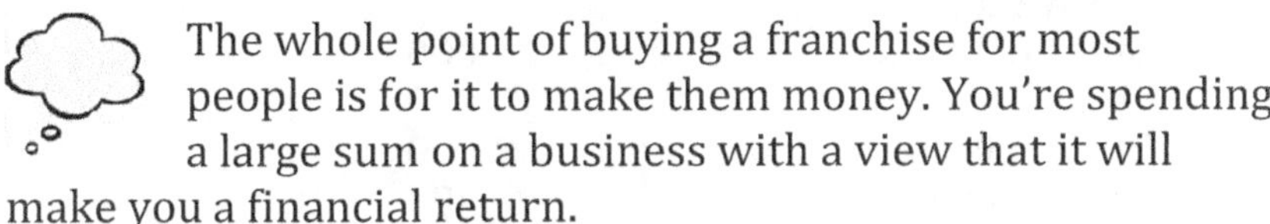 The whole point of buying a franchise for most people is for it to make them money. You're spending a large sum on a business with a view that it will make you a financial return.

The underlying problem is, that you, nor anyone else can see into the future. Even in a regular year (I'm writing this in 2020 as we move into our fifth month of lockdown) no one can predict what will happen to the economics in your country.

It's not all doom and gloom, however. There are certain things you can check to assess that all is reasonable.

Part 1 – A new franchise

The franchisor will provide you with a projection. It's prudent to start with the viewpoint that the projection is wrong. No one can see into the future. The questions to ask yourself is, were the assumptions behind the projection reasonable?

Here's what a typical income statement may look like:

Income statement of ABC Franchise

Turnover		120 000
Cost of sales:		
Opening stock	0	
Purchases	55 000	
Closing stock	(13 000)	
Total cost of sales		42 000
Gross profit		**78 000**
Gross profit % (margin)		65,00%
Overheads		
Staff costs	25 000	
Rent	15 000	
Electricity, rates and taxes	2 000	
Franchise fees	7 200	
Motor expenses	2 500	
Bank charges	800	
Point of sale system	1 200	
Internet	500	
Telephone	1 000	
Printing and stationery	2 000	
Insurance	1 000	
Uniform	1 000	
Total overheads		59 200
Net profit before tax		18 800
Tax at 28%		5 264
Profit after tax		**13 536**

 It's well worth doing some homework on the franchisor's projections. Remember, it's in their interests to present a healthy profit.

Ask to see the accounts for similar sized franchises in similar locations. This will give you a guide as to what similar stores are achieving.

Remember also that any new business can take a while to become established, so it may take some time for your franchise to reach its forecast turnover.

This is not an exact science, but here are some things you can consider about each line of the income statement.

1.1 Turnover

Break the turnover down. How much does it work out to per week, per day, per hour? Does it seem reasonable based on what you know about the business?

1.2 Gross profit

The percentage will come from the franchisor, but how does it compare to other franchises in the area, both the franchise you are looking at and other franchises in a similar industry?

1.3 Staff costs

The franchisor should be able to give a good idea of just how many staff you will need and their usual salary.

Consider how many hours your franchise will be open and whether that number of staff would be reasonable. A restaurant is likely to be open more hours and is more labour intensive than, say, a stationery shop.

1.4 Rent, Electricity, Rates and Taxes

Rent is a hugely variable cost depending on where your potential premises is located. A quick phone call to the landlord should be enough to confirm the cost of the premises.

There are many extra costs that can come with the rent though, some of them are obvious, some less so. It is worth checking with the landlord what extra costs they will pass on to you.

For example:
- Electricity
- Water
- Sewerage
- Rates and taxes
- Contribution to generator
- Parking
- Levies
- Contribution to upkeep of shared areas
- **Contribution to mall marketing**

1.5 Franchise fees

This isn't the one-off fee you pay to join the franchise. Your franchisor will charge you a percentage of your turnover in franchise fees. This is your cost for using their brand and may include such things as marketing contribution as well as a contribution towards the costs of the support team at head office.

Fees will vary from franchise to franchise but can range from 1% for low margin business to as high as 7% or even 8% for higher margin businesses.

But wait, I hear you say, the franchise fee is a direct cost of sales, shouldn't it be included as a cost of sales and so therefore reduce the gross margin percentage?

There is an argument to say that it should, but our experience was that it didn't form part of cost of sales. Make sure when comparing gross margins between franchises, you either exclude from all or include with all, that way the franchises are comparable.

1.6 Other costs:
The point of sale system will probably be determined by the franchisor and should be easy to cross reference against another franchisee's accounts
You should be able to obtain insurance/internet quotes easily enough.
Many of the other costs are subjective and will depend on the type of franchise you are looking at.

Part 2 – An existing franchise

 Can't I just use the bank statements of the existing franchise? That should give me an idea as to how profitable the business is.

The answer is – only partially. The bank statements will tell you what money has gone through the bank, but also consider:

- Is there a lot of cash business? Both expense and income that isn't banked.
- Is the owner putting any personal expenses through the bank account?
- Are there a lot of bills building up that haven't been paid? (creditors)
- Are there a lot of sales that haven't been paid for yet? (debtors)

 So, what about the accounts? You're buying an existing business so that business has a set of accounts, so we can just use those, right?

Well, yes and no. Clearly an actual set of results compared to a projection are likely to be more accurate, but remember the accounts are always prepared in arrears so they're historic and past performance is no guarantee of future performance.

What can I do to check the accounts? What is "due diligence"?

Put simply, due diligence checks to make sure that what you are being told by the current owners is correct. This is similar to an audit of the business you are buying. It will look at all aspects of the business and assess that the business is in good shape by:

- Checking the accounts are accurate.
- Looking at leases and contracts. Not just for the premises but other business services, for example telephones, point of sale, internet, vehicles and any marketing contracts.
- Checking ownership of assets.
- Is the business behind with its taxes? Is it behind with paying its suppliers?

Some professional firms will offer this as a service, but it will cost. However, it may be money well spent in the long term. Alternatively, you can assess for yourself, but make sure you ask to see the accounting records before you sign that purchase contract.

Part 3 – looking to the future

Whether you have existing accounts from the incumbent or a projection from the franchisor for a new franchise, it's a good idea to rework the numbers.

An even better idea is to have a number of projections prepared, so you can assess "what if?" for example:

What if my turnover is 15% below projection/last year?

What if my gross profit is 55% rather than 65%?

Will the franchise still give you a return big enough to live off?

 **Part 4 – break-even analysis**
Break even analysis looks at what your sales value will have to be so you don't make a loss. This is a useful exercise for target setting.

This you can calculate back by taking all your regular costs that don't change with turnover (these are called fixed costs), and then dividing back by your gross margin.

Let's look back at our income statement again (on the next page). I've added a column to look at the costs by type:

Income statement of ABC Franchise			Type of cost
Turnover		120 000	
Cost of sales:			
Opening stock	0		
Purchases	55 000		
Closing stock	(13 000)		
Total cost of sales		42 000	Variable (varies
Gross profit		**78 000**	dependent on turnover)
Gross profit % (margin)		65,00%	
Overheads			
Staff costs	25 000		Fixed *
Rent	15 000		Fixed
Electricity, rates and taxes	2 000		Fixed **
Franchise fees	7 200		Variable
Motor expenses	2 500		Fixed **
Bank charges	800		Fixed **
Point of sale system	1 200		Fixed
Internet	500		Fixed
Telephone	1 000		Fixed **
Printing and stationery	2 000		Fixed **
Insurance	1 000		Fixed
Uniform	1 000		Fixed **
Total overheads		59 200	
Net profit before tax		18 800	
Tax at 28%		5 264	
Profit after tax		**13 536**	

* There may be some variable elements - for example overtime
** Mainly fixed, but maybe some small variation based on turnover

For the basis of this exercise, let's assume that the "mostly" fixed costs are completely fixed and there's no overtime. The total costs that we have to cover total are 59,200 (the total

overheads figure from the income statement) less 7,200
(franchise fees) = 52,000.

Our gross profit margin is 65% so our cost of sales are 35%.
The franchise fees are at 6%, so total variable costs are 41%.

The turnover we need to make is therefore 52,000 divided by
59% (1 less 41%) = 88,100 (rounded).

Why is it useful to know my breakeven number?
The last thing you want to do is to make a loss. By taking your
breakeven point, you can track by day or by sales volume how
you are doing during the month.

Part 5 – Seasonality – what is it?
Seasonality simply means that some months will
naturally be better trading months than others.
There are a variety of different reasons for this, for example:
- Holiday season – businesses in Johannesburg in
  December are naturally quiet as many people hit the
  coast. Conversely, tourist destinations will be busier.
- Restaurants will be busier in December with work
  holiday parties.
- Automotive business may well be busier around
  vacation time as holidaymakers make sure their cars
  are roadworthy before going away.

Seasonality and your cash-flow
Keep in mind which months you are busy and which
months you are not, you may need to put cash away
to cover those quiet months. (It's always worth putting cash
aside for unforeseen circumstances).

Remember also that your monthly expenditure will not occur at the same time during the month as your monthly income. Income can come in at any time during the month, but:

- Your rent is likely to be due on the first of the month,
- Your salaries will be due around the end of the month,
- Your franchise fees will also have a fixed due date.

Plan your cash-flow accordingly.

Part 6 – Value Added Tax (VAT) aka sales tax

6.1 What is it?

This is a tax added onto most goods and services.

Many countries in the world have some form of VAT (often called GST). At the time of writing, Hungary has the world's highest VAT rate at 27%. Some other world rates are:

- South Africa – 15%
- The UK – 20%
- The USA – 10%

6.2 How does it work?

You add the VAT onto the cost of the goods. For example, if your sales price of a stapler is 100 and you're in South Africa, then you charge the customer 115 (100 + 15%).

At the end of the VAT period which may be 1, 2 or 3 months (varies by country – South Africa is typically every 2 months), you add up all the VAT you have charged your customers, then deduct all the VAT you have spent on your costs and pay the difference over to the revenue service in your country. It's worth taking advice though, because not all the VAT you spend will be recoverable, for example on business entertaining.

In this way, you are effectively working as a tax collector.

6.3 Do I have to register for VAT?

Some countries (including South Africa) have rules in place so you only register when you are above a certain rate of annual turnover. If you're below that annual level of turnover then you don't have to register.

6.4 How does it affect me?
6.4.1 Admin

VAT is an administrative burden. You have to maintain accurate records (you should be doing this anyway) and you will have to submit VAT returns on time. There will be fines for late returns.

6.4.2 Cashflow

You will need to bear in mind that all the VAT you collect from your customers legally **IS NOT YOURS**. Don't spend it, you have to pay that money over. You may think you have more cash in the bank than you actually have.

Remember also that you will have to pay VAT on your expenses. When you agree a lease, it is likely that your rent quoted will be the pre-VAT figure. You will be able to recover the VAT, but you have to pay it to your landlord first.

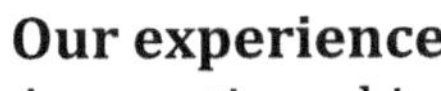

Our experience

As mentioned in chapter 7, we were never able to get our gross margin high enough and as a consequence we struggled to cover our costs.

We did put money away from the daily takings to cover the salaries at the end of the month, but often it was touch and go.

We didn't fully appreciate the seasonality aspects and suffered when the major school holidays meant that many people went away – that meant that March/April and December/January were extremely bad months for us.

I did perform some financial due diligence myself. The numbers I looked at did not support the numbers as presented in the accounts. I looked in July, the accounts were for the year ended February. I should have taken more notice, but having put the time in, I felt emotionally involved and wanted my findings to be wrong.

With hindsight I should have been more objective and trusted my findings.

Chapter review

In this chapter we've looked at:

- How to look at costs objectively to assess estimates/accounts,
- Breakeven analysis, what is it and why is it useful?
- Seasonality and how it may impact your business,
- VAT and its impact on your business.

Chapter 9 - Staff

Love 'em or loathe them, your franchise is more than likely going to need at least some staff to run it. Be it cooks, waiters, delivery drivers, mechanics or sales consultants a good staff member is worth their weight in gold. A poor staff member may not only turn your customers away but give your franchise a bad reputation, losing you future business and incurring the wrath of your franchisor.

Paperwork
Whether you buy an existing franchise or you're setting up a new one, be prepared for paperwork. Some of the list below is specific to South Africa, but there're likely to be similar requirements in your country:
- Contracts of employment/performance criteria
- Work visas (for foreign nationals)
- Unemployment Insurance Fund (UIF)
- Workmans Compensation
- IRP5's and IT3A's
- Bonus pay/commission structures
- Pension contributions/provident fund
- Union fees

Employing staff - existing franchise
Don't be afraid to ask the current owners who the bad apples are. Look at their personnel records and any warnings issued.

Ensure that the staff know that those warnings will be carried forward. Before you take over, you can insist the existing owner removes the bad apples.

Employing staff - new franchise
You're reliant on the interview process and collecting references from previous bosses. Make sure that new staff are given trial periods and watch them carefully during the franchisor training.

MAKE SURE YOU OPERATE WITHIN THE LAW.

Your staff have rights and they probably know them better than you do. Take time to research the proper disciplinary procedure and make sure you stick to it. Be a fair boss, but at the same time be ruthless when applying the rules.

I'm not a labour lawyer, but I do recommend you take a good labour lawyer's advice.

How much is a staff member going to cost me?
Don't think that they will only cost their salary, overtime and commission. There are also additional costs involved in employing staff. The following deductions from your employee's pay also require a mandatory employer contribution:

- Unemployment Insurance Fund (UIF).
- Skills Development Levy (SDL).
- Workmans Compensation.

Optional deductions from your employees pay may also require a contribution from the employer:

- Provident fund.
- Medical aid.

These lists are specifically for South Africa, but many other countries will have similar (maybe additional) employer contributions.

Training - existing franchise

Make sure you find out when the staff were last trained. Franchises may insist on periodical refresher training. It may be the same training that you went on, so it's worth assessing the training as you're on it.

Training - new franchise

All your staff will need to be trained. This is a good way for you to assess how they work under pressure and their attitude.

Our experience

Our existing franchise came with more than a dozen staff. The incumbent was "babysitting" the business for an absent brother and knew very little and was willing to share even less.

With the benefit of hindsight, we should have taken the opportunity of the change of ownership to clear out at least three members of staff.

There was little paperwork in terms of staff performance, contracts or warnings and that should have been a warning to us to the previous owner's incompetence and the incompetence of the franchisor who should have ensured that these things were kept up to date during their (frankly intrusive and pointless) quarterly reviews.

One of our best members of staff was previously employed at the same franchise down the road. We met her during our training, where she was being trained into a manager.

For some reason, the franchisor had taken a disliking to her and said we shouldn't hire her. We hired her anyway and it was the best recruitment we ever did. The moral is that you have to work with your staff, so hire staff you want to work with.

When we took over, the franchisor told us the staff all had to be sent on refresher courses. This was at our expense and left us short-staffed at a time when we knew very little and needed the benefit of their experience.

The training we received, I believe, was flawed in three key areas:

1. Part of the training included studying for a memory based written test. This was an utter waste of time and thoroughly ineffective – why should I care about the history of the franchise? Why do I need to commit things to memory, when there are printed reminders in the kitchen?

2. The rest of the training was hands on, which was useful. The absence of any training about how to run a business or understanding the admin was not.

3. The staff received no training on how to deal with telephone orders, a key aspect of the business. There was limited training on the point of sale system and no script for the staff to follow to ensure smooth customer service. Then the franchisor asked why the sales consultants weren't upselling. The reason – they hadn't been trained to!

Chapter summary

- Staff are one of your key assets.
- Make sure they are well trained.
- Understand your commitments under payroll and employment law and comply with the applicable rules.
- Staff cost more than just their salary, overtime and commission.
- Be firm but fair.

Chapter 10 – Why some franchises fail

Having invested all that time, money, effort, blood sweat and tears into your franchise, the last thing you want is to have it fail. You want that investment to flourish and pay you a decent return.

So, why do some franchises fail?
This list is not exclusive just to franchises, many of the points made apply just as much if you were to set up your own small business.

10.1 Franchisor failure
It sounds obvious, but if the franchisor fails, then the franchisees will topple like a house of cards. Or a chain of dominoes. You may pick your favourite metaphor here.

Why would the franchisor fail? They're the ones with all the knowledge, right?

Possibly, but here are some reasons why your franchisor may fail:
- New franchisors with untried business models,
- Existing franchisors with out of date models,
- Franchisors not keeping up to date with technology or trends in the market place,
- Bad publicity.
- Lack of focus, be it on their product or on the market.

10.2 Franchisee failure

If you can't blame the franchisor, here are some things within your control to look out for:

10.2.1 Wrong franchise for you

Sometimes that franchise is just wrong. Although you loved that product as a consumer, for some reason you just can't put that passion into running that franchise. Ask yourself, is this your true passion and purpose?

10.2.2 Planning

Pathetic planning prevents perfect performance, or if you prefer, fail to plan is planning to fail.

Business plans are important. They are the map for the future of your franchise. A good franchisor should insist you have one, preferably one that is aligned to their business plan (our franchisor did not insist on this). The advantages of a business plan are:

- They give you an overview of your entire business,
- Set priorities,
- Manage change,
- Manage cashflow,
- Set milestones to monitor along the way,
- Help your memory. Why are you doing what you're doing – there is a purpose to it,
- Are your expectations realistic? A plan will help you see in black and white what can be done and what can't be done.

I've mentioned in chapter 5 that preparing a business plan would take a whole other book, so my advice is to get a professional on board to assist.

10.2.3 Running out of cash

This is probably one of the most obvious things I've written in this book, but it's majorly important. If you run out of cash, you can't pay suppliers so you have nothing to sell, you can't pay your rent or your staff.

How do I avoid running out of cash? Here's some ideas:

- Have a plan. How much cash do I need? (see chapter 8 for breakeven analysis).
- Put cash away for a rainy day.
- Reinvest in your business. Put spare money into marketing, new equipment, great stock.
- Monitor your stock carefully. Don't have too much cash tied up in stock that can go out of date/out of fashion quickly.
- Keep and maintain accurate accounting records. I can't stress this enough – you need to know who owes you money and what money you owe. Compare your accounts to your plan – where are you overspending?
- Are your staff stealing from you? (see chapter 7).
- (And yes, you can borrow. I don't recommend it).

10.2.4 Turning the spotlight on yourself

Yes, the cause of failure might be you. I know you don't want to hear that, (who does?) but consider:

- Are you motivated?
- Are you challenged?
- Is this your true calling, your passion, your purpose?
- Are you taking too much out of the business? Stock or cash?
- Are you staying on top of your accounts?
- Are you taking shortcuts in the system? The reason that some franchises are very successful is that they have tried and tested systems, techniques and

processes. Trying to circumvent these for the sake of convenience or a small cost saving may be a false economy.

10.2.5 Are you selling something people want to buy?
This is technically both the franchisor and a franchisee's responsibility, but sometimes you have to evolve in order to provide a service people want. Just think about your local DVD rental store in an age where downloading is so popular.

10.2.6 Training and staff
As mentioned in chapter 9, well trained staff that are knowledgeable and motivated will give the customer a great experience. The opposite is true for badly trained staff.

In all probability, franchises fail because of a combination of the above, rather than just one in isolation.

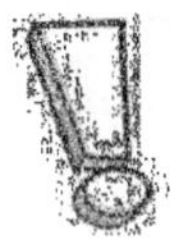

Our experience
As much as we would love to lay the blame entirely at the hands of our franchisor, we have to be realistic.
Looking back on our time in our franchise, there is no doubt that several of the above contributed to our failure.
We chose the wrong franchise in the beginning. We weren't prepared for the amount of work that was involved.
We didn't plan enough and eventually we ran out of cash.

Chapter summary
This chapter is designed to give you a heads up on why some franchises have failed in the past. Do your research on both the franchisor, franchisee and yourself.

Chapter 11 – Other things to consider

 This chapter is a catch-all of all the other things you may want to consider before buying a franchise and is based on our experience:

11.1 Training

As I mentioned in chapter 9, training is exceptionally important. It shouldn't just be how to do the work, but it should include some aspects of managing a business. If this is your first time in charge, there's huge amounts to learn. Consider taking a course in small business management to supplement your front-line training offered by the franchisor.

11.2 Unless you are a lawyer, you're not a lawyer

If you are spending hundreds of thousands or even millions on a franchise, be sure to spend a few thousand with a good lawyer who can review the franchise agreement so you know your rights as a franchisee. Knowledge is power and it will be worth every penny in the long run. It will pay you not to place too much trust in the franchisor, they may have their best interests at heart, not yours.

11.3 Know thy franchisor

You will likely have a close working relationship with someone from the franchisor's office. It may be a regional manager, brand manager or operations manager or even something else. Get to know that person. Can you work with them? What are they like? Are they motivated? Remember, this is the person you will go to with complaints and this is the person who will be passing complaints on to you.

11.4 Head office

How does head office look and feel? You may learn a lot about how the franchise is run from the location, layout and staff attitude of its head office. Find out what staff they have to assess what level of support you will get. Are the staff experts in what they do?

11.5 Churn, baby churn

Try to find out what the churn rate is – that is how many franchisees have re-sold their franchise. That will help you determine the success rate of the franchise. If many franchisees are looking to sell, or the franchise has fewer stores than it used to have, it may not be a good sign.

11.6 Be humble

Try to understand that if previous franchise owner/s struggled, it may not have been because they were an idiot. More likely it was a combination of reasons from chapter 10.

11.7 Store audits

Franchisors will visit stores and assess them, to ensure good standards are being met. Ask to see the last few audits for the store if you're buying an existing franchise.

11.8 Be careful of advice

Be careful if the franchisor gives you advice on the branch you are buying. This happened to us and yet it transpired that the branch hadn't been visited by the franchisor for well over a year, so couldn't possibly have an up to date picture of the store dynamics.

11.9 Don't toss out the rulebook
Your franchisor should have well documented processes in place to ensure that your performance meets their criteria. It is well worth investing some time to read this to make sure you are following their processes, especially if you're buying an existing franchise where current staff may have bad habits.

11.10 Specials can cost more than you think
This is especially true for the food industry, where franchisors run specials during quiet times, you as the franchisee will bear the cost of whatever is being offered free – thus cutting in to your profits.

11.11 Keep it balanced
Franchisors will generally keep the things they tell you about the franchise positive. They want you to buy the franchise. Keep this in mind when you talk to them.

11.12 What could go wrong?
You're excited and looking at the opportunities, but never lose sight of what could go wrong. This will keep you balanced and in touch with reality, rather than getting carried away with a fantasy.

11.13 It's a fine thing
Check if the franchisor issues fines, what they issue fines for, how much the fines are? Then find out when they last issued a fine and what they issued a fine for, but also speak to that franchise owner to determine fairness. When we first heard about this, it came as a surprise.

11.14 Administration time

Businesses require a lot of admin, and unless you're in a position to hire someone to do this for you, that task will fall on your shoulders. If you're running a busy franchise then this will often have to take place in what used to be your relaxation time.

11.15 Are you right for them?

Does a franchisor mind if you're not the right person for them? Are they just happy to increase/keep their footprint of outlets?

11.16 At the end

If it turns out not to be right for you and you end up selling your franchise, make sure you receive all the money from the buyer before you hand the keys over.

Chapter summary
This was a catch all of everything else we could think of from our personal experience. The key things are:

- Make sure this is your passion.
- Pay a lawyer to look over the contract.
- Be prepared to put in extra time for administration

Chapter 12 – Conclusion and top 5 do's and don'ts

Overview
In summary, throughout this book we've covered:
- What is a franchise?
- How does a franchise compare to starting your own business?
- How does buying a new franchise compare to existing franchise?
- How to assess the financial results of a new and existing franchise?
- Why franchises fail.

There is no doubt that franchises are incredibly popular and likely to become more so, and they can be richly rewarding both financially and emotionally. They can also be extremely hard work, emotionally and financially draining.

In summary, these are my top 5 do's and don'ts when deciding whether to invest in a franchise:

Do:
1.   Do choose carefully. Pick a franchise you have some knowledge/passion/interest in.
2.   Do pick the right location for your franchise.
3.   Do take time to understand the financials.
4.   Do research, research, research. Look for online reviews, speak to existing franchisees across a range of businesses and try to speak to people who have sold their franchises. Understand what they are going through. Why are they selling their franchise (if applicable)? How do they feel about their franchisor? Would they do it again?
5.   Do fully understand you rights and obligations per your franchise contract.

Don't:
1.   Don't rush into anything. Don't jump in because you're worried you might miss "that" opportunity. Another will come along.
2.   Don't pay the full asking price for an existing franchise.
3.   Don't think that you'll have more free time as a franchisee. Running your own franchise is hands-on, unless you have trusted staff, and then there's all that admin to do.
4.   Don't believe what you are told by the franchisor. Do your own research.
5.   Don't think you'll be able to buy a franchise and leave the staff to run it.

Chapter 13 – Jargon

Accounts – a financial summary of a business consisting of (amongst other things) an income statement and a balance sheet.

Asset – items owned that can be converted to cash, or cash itself. For example vehicles, computers, stock.

Balance sheet – a summary of assets and liabilities at a point in time, usually the financial year end of the business.

Brand – a symbol or logo used by a company to distinguish itself from its competitors.

Cost of sales – the total cost to produce and distribute the goods for sale.

Economies of scale – the concept that as you spend more, you receive better value for money.

Franchise – use of a company brand, processes and knowhow, usually for a fee.

Franchisee – the person using the business brand (that's you).

Franchisor – the owner of the brand/business.

Gross profit – turnover less cost of sales.

Income statement – a summary of trading income and expenses for a period of time – usually a year.

Liability – monies owed to third parties, for example suppliers or bank loans.

Net profit – the surplus revenue after deducting all costs.

Supplier – someone who provides you with goods and services.
Turnover (revenue) – value of total sales, excluding sales tax.
VAT/sales tax – a tax levied on the sale of items.